MANAGING CONFLICTS AT WORK

Diffuse tense situations and resolve arguments amicably

Written by Claude Matoux

Translated by Rebecca Neal

Coaching 50MINUTES.com

CONFLICT RESOLUTION

- **Problem:** how can you get rid of a toxic atmosphere in your workplace? What can you do to overcome your own negative reactions, as well as those of your colleagues and superiors?
- **Uses:** conflictual situations, including minor friction, disagreements, misunderstandings and even outright animosity, are part of our daily lives, both at home and at work. Learning to analyse them and (re)act more constructively will contribute to a more pleasant atmosphere at work.
- **Professional context:** relationships between colleagues, relationships with your team, relationships with superiors.
- **FAQs:**
  - Is conflict always a bad thing?
  - How should I deal with task-related conflict?
  - How should I deal with people-related conflict?
  - How can I tell if something is not right?
  - How can I resolve a conflict without one person losing?
  - How important are working conditions?

We may not like it, we may do everything we can to avoid it, but it often breaks out all the same.

Whenever we get a job, we dream of a "good working environment", just like we all dream of blue skies. However, stress, demotivation and aggressiveness are increasingly present in teams. Conflict is inevitable in human relationships, and it is useful to know how it progresses so that we can nip it in the bud.

Is conflict necessarily a bad thing for a company? Like stress, we tend to see it as something negative. However, just as we can distinguish between good stress, which is a driving force, and bad stress, which harms us, we can view conflict positively, as an opportunity for innovation and development, or negatively, when it poisons the atmosphere.

The more attention you pay to signs of discontent, the quicker you will be able to understand and manage them... to the extent that it is your responsibility. Indeed, the roots of conflict can be found at various different levels of a company. If it comes from the institution or organisation (such as a change in working hours or production norms), you will need to evaluate how much room for manoeuvre you have. If it comes from an unpleasant remark from a colleague, you have the freedom to act. If you are leading a team, it is your duty to keep the peace between team members and to maintain an atmosphere of trust and a feeling of fairness.

Conflicts can hurt us, cause us stress and make us ill. They make us cynical, aggressive and withdrawn. When an interpersonal conflict arises, it is important to put your emotions aside and find a win-win solution. If only one person wins, the conflict is not resolved, it is just silenced.

Are you more of an actor or a spectator? When you witness power struggles, open conflict, hostile emails, unpleasant comments or catfights, how do you react? Do you avoid the situation? Face up to it? Enter the fray? Put up with it? Take part? It is important to understand how you work and know yourself well if you want to act in a way that is more mature and respectful of the other person and their point of view.

When we go to the office, it is mainly so that we can work, produce things or carry out tasks, generally while interacting with other people. In spite of what Facebook would have us believe, we cannot become friends with a single click: your colleagues are your collaborators, not your friends. You need to stay professional at work under all circumstances, or you risk letting your emotions govern your behaviour. It is better to be open to dialogue and work towards your shared objectives.

> Sabrina greets Catherine very coldly. The new hire does not have the same qualifications as Sabrina, who therefore thinks that she is incompetent. "I don't have anything against you, but I don't think it's right that you're doing the same work as me." The company culture at their law office expects employees to be friendly and informal with one another. This leads to an awkward situation: should Catherine be friendly towards someone who is hostile to her, or should she draw attention to the conflict by being openly unfriendly? After a shaky start, this situation turned out well: Sabrina and Catherine were passionate about a shared project, threw themselves into it and were recognised for their hard work. Now, they are happy to greet each other warmly in the mornings. This shows that it is possible to overcome conflict at work without holding a grudge.

MANAGING CONFLICTS: THE BASICS

RECOGNISING A CONFLICT

Conflicts are a common and unavoidable occurrence in the world of work. They arise when the concerns of two or more seem impossible to reconcile.

- All conflicts have a minimum of two parties: two people, two teams, two groups, a person and a group, and so on.
- All conflicts are caused by a threat or a struggle, which can be either real or imagined.
- All conflicts result from interaction between people.
- Most conflicts are emotionally charged.

Cognitive conflict or relationship conflict?

- Cognitive conflict is related to the object of the conflict. It involves a clash of ideas and is an opportunity for innovation and development. It is often beneficial to teams and companies.
- Relationship conflict is linked to the relationship between the people involved. Power and emotions are at the heart of this type of conflict. The object is unimportant and there is therefore no point focusing on it to find a solution – that will only make things worse! This is the type of conflict we are going to focus on.

The components of conflict

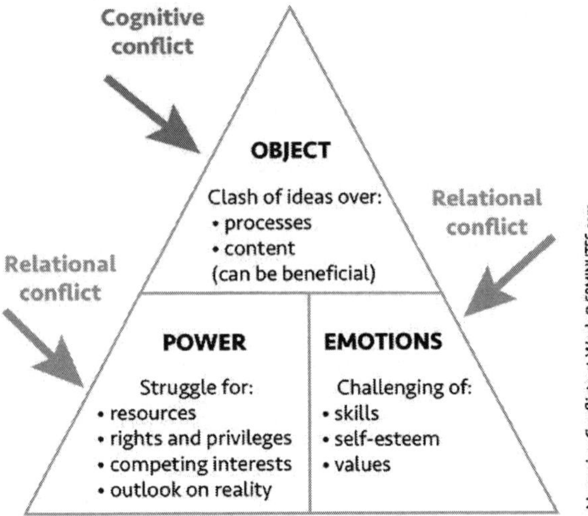

The sources of relationship conflicts

There are many reasons for relationship conflicts.

- **Information and facts:** your colleague has information that they do not pass on to you; your boss prioritises objectives that you think should be secondary; your supervisor evaluates you based on criteria that has little to do with your reality on the ground.
- **Resources:** your colleague has been given new equipment and is praised for completing tasks quickly while

you struggle with your old PC; you do not have time to complete all your tasks.
- **Competing interests:** your colleague has their eye on the same promotion as you; your supervisor suggests new working hours that you are not happy about; your colleague wants to open the window even though you are already cold.
- **Values:** your boss never says hello to you; your colleague is completely set in their ways; another colleague never takes part in social events.

Conflict as a process

All interpersonal communication implies a relationship between the emitter and the receiver. Conflict emerges within the relationship. Since relationships are not static, the conflict may gradually get worse or, conversely, fade by itself and end in peace.

There are five stages to conflict, from mere irritation to all-out war:

- accumulation (frustration, resentment);
- controlled indifference (tensions, reluctant communication);
- avoidance (reduced interaction);
- cold war (subtle attacks, forming alliances);
- open war (accusations and complaints).

As you can see, the sooner you take steps to resolve the conflict, the more likely you are to deal with it successfully.

POSSIBLE REACTIONS TO CONFLICT

How can you go about dealing with conflict? Although we may react differently depending on the conflict, we all favour a type of strategy depending on the situation. Two factors determine a person's approach to conflict management:

- their motivation to defend their interests;
- their motivation to cooperate with the other person.

The intersection of these two tendencies results in five ways of reacting to conflict.

Reactions to conflict

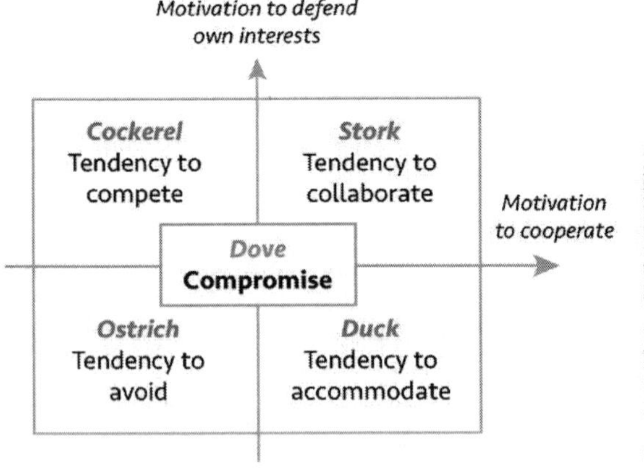

The ostrich

The ostrich chooses to avoid conflict at all costs by burying their head in sand. They would rather give up their personal interests than risk expressing their disagreement. They become uncomfortable at the first sign of tension and would rather back down than deal with confrontation.

Ostriches have no hope of resolving conflicts. Their strategy involves avoiding them.

The cockerel

The cockerel favours their own interests, even if this means forcing their partners to accept their conditions. Their objectives take priority over other people's needs. They want to win at all costs and have no qualms about intimidating, dominating or pushing out their rivals.

Cockerels have a black and white view of the world, according to which people are either dominant or dominated. This means that they work to make sure that they are winners. They find conflict stimulating. Their strategy involves constantly competing with the people around them.

The duck

Ducks want to be accepted and liked. They are always afraid of upsetting other people and are even prepared to give up their own interests to maintain good relationships. They tend to always say "yes", even if they are thinking "no". Ducks know that people sometimes take advantage of their kindness, but they persuade themselves that they were happy to help.

Ducks are afraid of conflict because they think that it harms personal relationships and the harmony of the team at work. Their strategy is to give in.

The stork

Storks care about both their interests and their relationships with other people. They try to find win-win solutions and to determine and reach shared goals. Storks want to work in an atmosphere of trust and mutual respect.

Storks therefore view conflicts positively, as they see them as an opportunity to improve work and help people to get on better. Their strategy is to collaborate.

The dove

Doves value dialogue. They are prepared to let go of some of their interests and know how to set out their arguments to other people so that they will do the same. They communicate in order to reach an agreement.

Doves face up to conflict and discuss it, with the aim of finding a peaceful solution that respects all parties. Their strategy involves looking for compromise.

RESOLVING CONFLICT WITH NO LOSERS

Communication above all

No conflict management involving domination and coercion can succeed in the long term. Using force will only fuel the person's frustration and feeling that they are not understood. Managing conflicts constructively necessarily involves collaboration or compromise.

In all conflicts, the people involved believe that they are in the right and, consequently, that their position is the legitimate one. You cannot resolve the conflict without both parties being at least partially satisfied. This means that you will have to communicate. Conflict resolution requires communication to express the conflictual situation and the issues for the different parties, and negotiation to arrive at a mutually acceptable solution. Below are five effective communication tools for resolving conflict.

DESC script

This technique is used to communicate sensitive messages: telling a colleague that you disagree with them, bringing someone back into line, announcing a transfer or a dismissal, and so on.

- **D for "describe":** be precise and factual. Avoid generalisations like "always" and "never" and approximations like "often" and "I've heard". Remain objective. The facts must be indisputable and verifiable.
- **E for "express":** state your emotion or feeling with complete sincerity.
- **S for "specify":** suggest a realistic solution.
- **C for "consequences":** make a connection between the concrete suggestion and a positive, motivating prospect.

Daniel and Peter used to get on well, and they worked together pleasantly and effectively. However, ever since Daniel was promoted to manage the team, Peter has been treating him differently. Daniel feels challenged and ignored when he suggests ways of working. He decides to set up a face-to-face meeting with Peter.

D – "Peter, for the last two weeks you've rejected all my work suggestions at the weekly team meeting. I've noticed this opposition since I was made project manager."

E – "I want to let you know that I feel disappointed and angry. I'm disappointed because I enjoyed working with you in the past and angry because I feel as though I'm being treated as an enemy."

S – "I am asking you to consider our shared projects and to put the wellbeing of the team and the company first."

C – "I want to be able to count on you and your skills. That will be best for all of us."

With DESC scripts, the essential thing is to assert yourself without putting the other person down and to adopt appropriate body language.

Empathy

Empathy is your ability to put yourself in another person's shoes. It is a natural capacity that you can develop in order to make the person you are talking to less hostile. On the other hand, if you are not empathetic, they are likely to be more hostile!

As conflict often stems from a difference in points of view, showing the other person that you are capable of understanding their viewpoint will tend to diffuse the situation. Below are some tips to become more empathetic:

- Express your empathy: "I understand that you are disappointed."
- Reformulate what the other person has just said: "I understand that you wanted to go to the training session."
- Acknowledge the other person's needs: "I know that it would have been useful for you."
- Specify your own needs: "We're understaffed and I need you to be there so that we can get the order out on Friday."
- Tell them that you might have reacted in the same way: "In your place, I'd have been disappointed as well."
- Create a positive link with the future: "You will be a priority for the next training session."

Active listening

In conflicts, each party sticks to their point of view and is convinced that they are right. If everyone stands their ground and refuses to listen to other people, it will be impossible to find common ground. Listening to the other person does not mean "agreeing with their way of seeing things", but rather "listening to their opinion in order to find a compromise".

> The parable of the blind men and the elephant tells of a prince who was travelling through a land populated by blind men on the back of an elephant, an animal which had never been seen there. Three blind men were chosen to touch the strange animal and describe it to the others. The first blind man, who had only touched the elephant's ear, explained that the animal resembled a coarse rug beaten by the wind on a washing line. The second man, who had only touched the trunk, said that it was a kind of very thick and very lively snake. The third man, who had only touched a leg, told the others that it was a beast as massive and calm as a tree. The blind men came to blows because they all thought that they were right and that the others were liars.

Wisdom lies in recognising that you can only see one side of the story: your view of reality is necessarily subjective and distorted by a number of filters, namely your background, your experiences, your personality, your thoughts and your emotions. Communicating will enable you to broaden your outlook and, like in the parable, have a more accurate view of reality. It is especially useful to listen to the other person's position because, if you fail to do so, you will often ascribe negative intentions to them.

Active listening is a powerful tool. "All" it requires is some open-mindedness, at least for the dialogue phase. Conversely, being unable or unwilling to listen to the other person's point of view can be seen as violent. Experience shows that it is often possible to resolve a conflict without even needing to negotiate if both parties are able to express themselves and listen to the other party.

"I" expressions

Obviously, accusations need to be avoided in conflict management. Banish "you", which is often loaded with criticisms and judgement, from your vocabulary: "You're annoying me. You don't understand. You shouldn't do that. You don't listen."

Conversely, "I" expresses how you are feeling and reassures the person you are talking to: "I'm tired. I want to understand. I think you'll do better if you write legibly. I'd like your attention."

Talking in the first person is often difficult for people who were taught not to talk about themselves and show off. Tell yourself that you are expressing your feelings and opinions, not praising yourself. Above all, this approach is about honesty and nonaggression.

TEST: WHAT WORDING DO YOU PREFER?

- "You need to get here on time" or "I'm counting on you being here at 8"?
- "You're stopping me from working" or "I need some quiet to concentrate on my work"?
- "You need to finish this report by 3" or "I need this report before the client gets here at 3"?

By using expressions with "I", you will avoid the conflicts that could arise when the other person feels that you are accusing them. We generally dislike being ordered around, so try not to do it to other people!

Assertiveness

Assertiveness is an ideal mode of communication and is well suited to conflict management. This behaviour involves being neither passive nor aggressive: in other words, you respect yourself and other people.

If you are determined and aware of your own value, you will not be afraid of other people's judgement. You will then be able to assert your needs and opinions. Rather than wishing that people were different, you can welcome discussion and put your point across firmly and politely. Since you do not feel threatened, you can pay attention to your objectives while listening to the other side's arguments. You know that it is not the end of the world if you make a mistake. You are therefore not looking to catch flaws, but to move projects and ideas forward in order to get results.

NEITHER PASSIVE NOR AGGRESSIVE

To come across as confident, order your thoughts clearly and act with self-assurance. Ask open questions. Walk with energy. Stand up straight. Smile! Be specific and realistic. Talk about facts, not people: criticise the meal, not the cook.

CALMING A TEAM

The team leader's role involves organising, managing and driving the team. Depending on their management style, they will focus on the task, relationships or both. The harmony of the team, and therefore the management of conflicts, is part of their role. It is up to them to intervene if they are personally involved in a conflict with a member of their team, or if they notice an interpersonal conflict between two people or a group conflict, whether it arises within the group or between two groups.

The team leader must always keep in mind that some friction, as long as it is channelled well, can provide encouragement and promote change within the team. When the dialogue resulting from a conflict is managed well, it can increase the awareness and knowledge of the other person. Healthy questioning can release tension and result in innovative ideas.

As a team leader, you need to help the different sides to resolve their conflict; do not try to deal with it for them. You should get both sides to listen to each other. Encourage them to always talk about their needs, not their frustrations. Accusations should be avoided as far as possible. Make time for dialogue and silence, encourage the participants to reword their ideas and let solutions appear with as little intervention as possible. The outcome will be fairer and easier to accept if it comes from the people involved or the team than if it is imposed by a superior.

ADVICE FOR EMPLOYEES

Keep your manager informed about your needs. Have clear objectives and do not be afraid to say "no" if you can show that it is justified. A well-argued refusal is better than resentment or burnout!

TOP TIPS

- Even if other people are getting on your nerves, be aware that you cannot change them: your only way of improving your relationship is to modify your own behaviour. You should therefore be willing to do some self-analysis and take action.
- Be honest: at the first sign of tension, speak to the people involved. This will allow you to clarify the situation before it deteriorates. Above all, it will prevent contentious remarks from being exaggerated or twisted by third parties, and will stop people from taking sides or forming cliques.

SOMETHING TO AVOID

Do not communicate in writing if you are annoyed or angry. For example, avoid responding via email. If you have no other choice, do not use bold or underline, which will come across as extremely aggressive. Similarly, if you write in capitals and use exclamation marks, you may as well be shouting.

Never respond to an unpleasant email when you are emotional. Give yourself time to think and, if you feel the need, get a third party to reread your response. Do not forget that once you have put something in writing, you cannot take it back.

- Tell the people you are working with what you expect, what you are working on and what you know about upcoming changes in the company.

- Bring people together by taking into account the mission and objectives of the company and its partners. Speak constructively by highlighting the team's shared goals.
- Do not judge! Trying to be right will only increase tensions. Try to understand the other person's point of view by listening to them. Be curious about other people and open to their ideas.

- Pay attention to your emotions: take the distance you need to decide whether or not they are proportional to the situation. Take some time before you react if you need to.
- Develop a positive attitude. People will like and trust you more, and you will feel a lot better.

EXTRA INFORMATION

If you are seen as a positive person who knows how to give out compliments, people will be more willing to agree to your requests, even if they are demanding.

- Look after your personal balance and your mood by maintaining a healthy lifestyle. When you are healthy, relaxed and confident, you will have no reason to be aggressive towards others and you will not be affected by unpleasant comments.
- Keep your sense of humour! It keeps your relationships healthy and happy, and can help you out of even the most difficult situations. It is a magic ingredient, to be used sparingly and judiciously at work. However, do not confuse humour with sarcasm, which may be perceived as a form of aggression. Laughing is good for both your body and your mind.

FAQS

IS CONFLICT ALWAYS A BAD THING?

Not at all! Conflict arises regularly in our private and professional lives because people have different interests, which
inevitably clash at times. Conflict is therefore normal, and
expressing differences of opinion or goals is very healthy: it
is better to say it than to hold it in. This means that, as long
as it is resolved early enough and everyone's opinion is taken
into account, conflict can be a positive thing.

ADVICE FOR EMPLOYERS

Because people do not like them, conflicts are often
stifled. However, minimising the importance of conflict
or telling new employees that is forbidden is a big mistake! Even if you do not need to attach importance to
the first minor disagreement, it is essential to clear the
air when you notice tension.

HOW SHOULD I DEAL WITH TASK-RELATED CONFLICT?

A conflict linked to tasks, in other words to a precise object,
is a cognitive conflict. You should be happy, because if
a clash of ideas is handled well it can lead to innovations
which benefit the company. In this case, you need to use
negotiation techniques: deal with the difference of opinion

by focusing on shared interests and avoiding personal positions. Think of solutions in terms of mutual benefits and find an agreement based on objective criteria. Present the clash as an exchange that will galvanise the team.

HOW SHOULD I DEAL WITH PEOPLE-RELATED CONFLICT?

Get both sides to express their point of view as soon as possible in order to iron out the problem and, generally, to minimise it. When emotions are running high, keeping quiet tends to magnify contentious statements or exaggerate the importance of behaviour that is seen as uncalled for. In this case, there is no point trying to find the root of the conflict, because the aim is to defuse the situation and make a fresh start in an environment of renewed trust.

SOMETHING TO AVOID

You should absolutely avoid trying to find out who is right and who is wrong.

HOW CAN I TELL IF SOMETHING IS NOT RIGHT?

Obviously, verbal attacks, criticism and putting other people down can lead to conflict. A single hurtful phrase can stay indelibly printed on our memories for years. If a supervisor humiliates their employee by pointing out a mistake in a meeting, this can cause lasting resentment. Promoting the manager's favourite makes the rest of the team jealous. This is why you need to always be respectful and fair to everybody.

While verbal sparring is a very visible sign of conflict, avoidance is just as significant. In this case, the people involved do not behave aggressively, but opt for a strategy of evasion. When people only communicate if they absolutely have to, hide behind emails and avoid each other in the corridor, in meetings and at events, this a clear sign that tensions are simmering. It is easier to put out a small fire than a raging inferno...

HOW CAN I RESOLVE A CONFLICT WITHOUT ONE PERSON LOSING?

A conflict cannot be fully resolved if someone is left out. Rather than wanting to get rid of it as quickly as possible, it is therefore important to give it the consideration it deserves and take the time you need to deal with it. Think of this effort as an investment for the future. The rivalries that take hold, the demotivation that results and even burnout will be much costlier than the time taken to neutralise the conflict at the root.

First of all, the two parties need to be listened to and must listen to one other. Make sure that each person expresses themselves on their own behalf and explains how they see the situation, using "I" and without being aggressive towards the other person. Once both parties have expressed their position and their feelings, they should spontaneously suggest ways of moving past the conflict. It is a good idea to set clear markers so you can see the progress that has been made.

HOW IMPORTANT ARE WORKING CONDITIONS?

It would be wrong to suggest that conflicts only arise because of differences of interests or opinions, particular behaviours or differences in values. Other elements, such as precarious circumstances and differences in status and/ or salary within a team can also stir up jealousy and create tensions.

The working environment also determines the atmosphere within a team. How can an employee feel relaxed if they do not have enough space to maintain a feeling of wellbeing and safety? Unless these conditions are a necessary part of the job, how can a person feel happy in a dirty, drab, dark, noisy, bad-smelling, airless, freezing cold or overheated room? How can they avoid being irritated when their equipment is outdated or faulty? How can they work effectively when the IT system is constantly crashing?

Depending on the employer's budget, they should try to create a pleasant and comfortable workplace with an area to relax, somewhere to have lunch and places where it is possible to speak confidentially. In larger companies, management can encourage activities outside work to allow employees to get to know one another better, sporting activities to keep them healthy and allow them to relax, and wellbeing activities such as mindfulness meditation to enable them to maintain a sense of balance. It is in all companies' best interests to have satisfied, motivated and mentally and physically healthy staff who are happy to get up in the morning to go to a job that they enjoy. The working environment and the resources employed play a big part in this!

ADVICE FOR EMPLOYEES

While it is better and easier for the employer to create a healthy, calm, functional and comfortable environment for their team, you can still take steps to personalise your space. Some photos, personal items, lucky charms and plants will create a comforting, familiar space. You can also make suggestions about the décor – maybe nobody has thought about it yet! Some accessories to mark celebrations will also brighten up your workplace, and your colleagues will thank you for it.

OVER TO YOU

Think about the number of conflicts you have recently experienced at work and select five to describe briefly. For each one, identify the person or people involved and try to put your finger on the word, phrase or attitude that triggered the antagonism. Finally, ask yourself "What could I have done differently?" You may then be able to come up with useful solutions for every conflict.

Use the table below:

Over to you

CONFLICT	PERSON/ PEOPLE INVOLVED	TRIGGERS	ALTERNATIVE REACTION
1.			
2.			
3.			
4.			
5.			

We want to hear from you!
Leave a comment on your online library
and share your favourite books on social media!

FURTHER READING

BIBLIOGRAPHY

- Balestra, C. [Claudio], Bouancheaux Zuckermandl, É. and Balestra, C. [Constantino] (2014) *Introduction à la CommunicAction*. Brussels: La Charte Professional Publishing.
- Cormier, S. (2004) *Dénouer les conflits relationnels en milieu de travail*. Quebec: Presses de l'Université du Québec.
- Keller, F. (2013) *Pratiquer la CNV au travail*. Paris: InterEditions.
- Latendresse, J. (No date) Faire face aux conflits. *Centre 1,2,3 GO!* [Online]. [Accessed 30 June 2017]. Available from: <http://www.rqvvs.qc.ca/documents/file/faire-face-conflits.pdf>
- Rosenberg, M. (2003) *Dénouer les conflits par la communication non violente*. Thonex: Éditions Jouvence.
- Salomé, J. and Potie, C. (2000) *Oser travailler heureux*. Paris: Éditions Albin Michel.

ADDITIONAL SOURCES

- Cloke, K. and Goldsmith, J. (2011) *Resolving Conflicts at Work: Ten Strategies for Everyone on the Job*. Hoboken, New Jersey: John Wiley & Sons.
- Rosenberg, M. (2012) *Living Nonviolent Communication: Practical Tools to Connect and Communicate Skilfully in Every Situation*. Boulder, Colorado: Sounds True, Inc.

IMPROVE YOUR GENERAL KNOWLEDGE

IN A BLINK OF AN EYE !

www.50minutes.com

www.50minutes.com

Ebook EAN: 9782806269881

Paperback EAN: 9782806284624

Legal Deposit: D/2016/12603/400

Cover: © Primento

Digital conception by Primento, the digital partner of publishers.